SOUTH JUNCTION

DIESELS ON THE LONDON MIDLAND

56059

DIESELS
ON THE LONDON MIDLAND

JOHN VAUGHAN

LONDON

IAN ALLAN LTD

First published 1981

ISBN 0 7110 1146 X

Published by Ian Allan Ltd, Shepperton, Surrey; and printed by Ian Allan Printing Ltd at their works at Coombelands in Runnymede, England

Front cover: Class 45 No 45.024 seen near Appleby with a Carlisle-Nottingham train on 26 April 1980. *W. A. Sharman*

Back cover: Class 40 No 40.081 leaves Manchester Victoria with a train for Bangor in July 1980. *G. S. Cutts*

Introduction

The London Midland Region is the largest of the BR regions and to provide a full coverage of the diesel traction scene in both geographical and chronological terms in slightly more than 200 photographs is a difficult task. Over the years regional boundaries have changed substantially and the London Midland has inherited property, especially from the Western Region, from High Wycombe to Aberystwyth. The Region has boundaries from Clapham Junction in the south, to points near Newark and Sheffield in the east. Aberystwyth and Holyhead in the West and Gretna in the north. The diesel-hauled services on the Region are wide ranging and include main line expresses, heavy concentrations of freight traffic, cross-country and rural branch trains. Photographs of most areas have been included in this volume but inevitably some districts are covered more comprehensively than others. A total of 38 locomotive types or classes has been incorporated in the book plus a number of multiple units. Some, rarely photographed, experimental locomotives are illustrated in a single view while the ubiquitous Class 47s require some 27 pictures to do them justice. The London Midland Regional boundaries applied in this volume are those prevailing at the beginning of 1981.

The forerunner of the LM Region, the London Midland & Scottish Railway, was among the pioneers in British railway diesel traction, at least in terms of standardised classes. Experiments took place in the 1920s and in the 1930s a large number of diesel shunters were built for use on the LMS. Immediately after World War 2 discussions were held with what was left of British industry, and, although Southern Railway staff had visited the United States of America (where there was considerable experience in the field of diesel electric traction) with a view to building main line diesels in this country, it was the LMSR which was to lead the field. No 10000, built by the LMS in conjunction with English Electric was the first main line diesel for a British railway and appeared in December 1947 — just before the date of Nationalisation. The Chief Mechanical Engineer at the time, the late Mr H. G. Ivatt, must take much of the credit for venturing into what was, at least in the UK, the unknown. After Nationalisation, a sister locomotive, No 10001, was built and the analysis of the performance of these early main-liners was to prove most valuable when, in the 1955 Modernisation Plan, large-scale dieselisation was proposed. In the late 1950s and early 1960s a variety of manufacturers produced some weird and wonderful machinery, all hoping to win substantial orders from British Railways. Most examples are illustrated herein. Some had only a short life in service while others were the forerunners of what were to be classes of many hundreds of locomotives.

The London Midland Region is unique in that it has boundaries with every other Region on British Rail. Although the LMR does not have an allocation of all the BR diesel classes by virtue of this geographical 'contact', nearly all classes of diesel locomotive have worked on to the Region at some time or another. However, railway photographers have not always been on hand when rare workings have occurred, eg when Class 26 or 27 locomotives have occasionally worked into Carlisle. It is not the purpose of this volume to include illustrations of the many classes of electric locomotives and emus on the LMR.

Few of the photographs reproduced in this volume have been previously published and in the main these are instances where the subject matter is unusual and no other photographs are available. The wide coverage has only been made possible by including the work of over 60 photographers and to all those who submitted material, in some cases to have only a few of their photographs reproduced, I extend my sincere thanks and gratitude. The illustrations show scenes recorded between 1955 and 1980 with some emphasis on more recent times. The locomotives featured were introduced on the LMR between 1936 and 1980, a period of some 45 years. The locations shown in the photographs are as varied as the motive power and the reader will soon appreciate the diversity of LMR landscapes from the major stations of our great cities, to the coal mines of the East Midlands, the wilds of the Settle and Carlisle line, the remote shores of the Cambrian Coast and the quiet branch lines.

It is my wish that *Diesels on the London Midland* will afford the reader the opportunity of experiencing an 'armchair' Midland Railrover for a fraction of the real cost as well as reflecting the changing traction scene over a 25 year period. If I am successful in this and if the volume finds a permanent place on the enthusiast's bookshelf I shall be well satisfied. My thanks goes to my publishers for the freedom allowed to me in making the selection of photographs for inclusion and for making the contents of the Ian Allan Library available.

John A. M. Vaughan
Dorking, Surrey
May 1981

Shunting Classes

Above left: From the early 1930s the London Midland and Scottish Railway, the predecessor of the BR London Midland Region, had a number of small shunting locomotives. The variety of types was considerable and two of them are illustrated here. This is a 29ton machine with a 150bhp engine built by John Fowler in 1936. It was photographed at Nottingham in 1963 when in departmental stock.
Ian Allan Library (IAL)

Left: A much larger 350hp locomotive was this 0-6-0 from English Electric, introduced in 1939. They were built at Derby and turned the scales at over 54tons. This former LMS locomotive carried the BR No 12013 and was near the end of its days when photographed at Crewe South depot in March 1960. *A. Swain*

Above: Few would recognise this view of the old Birmingham New Street station taken in May 1964. A 204hp Gardner-engined 0-6-0 diesel mechanical shunter No D2395, later to be designated Class 03, stands between platforms 3 and 4 with a few wagons, while on the right a dmu waits to leave on a working to Redditch. *M. Mensing*

Right: This unusual photograph qualifies for inclusion because it shows an ex-BR 204hp shunter on an ex-London Midland Region branch line. The sometimes slightly eccentric activities of the railway fraternity included on this occasion an open coal wagon ride from Harpenden to Hemel Hempstead behind No D2207 on 7 August 1971.
Stanley Creer

Above: Coalville is now completely devoid of passenger services but coal trains can still be found in abundance. Shunting some vacuum-braked wagons in the up sidings is one of the ubiquitous Class 08 0-6-0s No 08.046. Once the train is formed a pair of Class 20s will take it to one of the many collieries in the area for loading. *Colin Marsden*

Left: An attractive view of 350hp English Electric-engined Class 08 No 08.877 crossing the Hope to Edale road at Earle's Cement Works in the Peak District's Hope Valley. The sidings see heavy traffic which leaves in both easterly and westerly directions on the adjacent main line. Photographed on 27 May 1980. *Roger Kaye*

Right: Class 08 shunters find regular employment in the Crewe Works of British Rail Engineering Ltd where the railway network is extensive. The locomotives are used to move stores and other railway vehicles (including locomotives in works for overhaul) around the complex. No 08.390 pauses between duties on 13 September 1979. *John Vaughan*

Centre right: A shunter at work at Gresty Wagon Shop, Crewe, in January 1980. With a light sprinkling of snow on the ground No 08.416 is being coupled to a line of mixed wagons under the overhead crane. *Barry J. Nicolle*

Below: It is still necessary for large stations to have a 'pilot' available for routine shunting. Carlisle normally has a Class 08 on hand to shunt a few parcels vans and less frequently a main line train. No 08.911 poses beside Nos 45.047 and 86.021, the latter on a Motorail train to Kensington, on 3 June 1977. *Brian Morrison*

Early Types and Experimental Locomotives

Left: A striking and previously unpublished photograph of No 10001, one of the well-known main line diesel twins built by the LMS at Derby Works in 1947. It could be said that they were the forerunners of the two hundred Class 40s, especially in respect of the 16 cylinder power unit. Under fine old semaphore signals the locomotive leaves Leighton Buzzard with the 09.10 Euston to Bletchley on 7 May 1955. *Stanley Creer*

Below left: Another type employing the 16-cylinder English Electric engine was the trio of 1Co-Co1 locomotives built for the Southern Region and for a time used by the London Midland. Also at Leighton Buzzard No 10202 leans to the curve with an up Wolverhampton train on 7 June 1958. *K. L. Cook*

Right: A curious machine built by the North British Locomotive Company was this 827bhp diesel-electric locomotive. Even during 1950 this power rating combined with a weight of almost 70tons would have put the machine in, at best, the mixed traffic category. No 10800 was pictured at Derby on 3 June 1958. *R. J. Buckley*

Centre right: A unique diesel-mechanical prototype built at Derby and introduced in 1951 was the 2-D-2 'Fell' locomotive No 10100. Its four 500bhp Paxman engines, two in each end, were arranged to operate individually so that the locomotive would start away on one engine and the No 2, 3 and 4 engines would come into gear automatically at pre-set road speeds. This novel concept was not particularly successful and it lasted only until 1957. This April 1955 view shows a 'two piece' coupling rod which effectively made the wheel arrangement 2-B-B-2. *P. H. Groom*

Below: During 1955 the prototype English Electric 'Deltic' appeared. British Railways provided facilities for the locomotive to be fully road tested but it remained the property of the manufacturer. The 3,300hp monster in striking blue livery performed for several years on LMR expresses and eventually led to an order being placed for 22 similar locomotives for use on the Eastern Region. Here with a train of LMS stock, *Deltic* waits to leave Liverpool Lime Street. *IAL*

Left: The experimental 'GT3' was a 4-6-0 gas turbine locomotive. Nevertheless this photograph taken near Leicester on crew training in 1961 was worth including in this section. Rated at 2,750hp the locomotive employed mechanical transmission through a gearbox but alas, like so many experimental machines, it did not fulfill expectations and was relegated to the scrap heap in 1966. *Colin P. Walker*

Below: One of the most successful experimental testbeds was undoubtedly DP2. The locomotive was introduced in 1962 and was tantamount to a Class 50 in Class 55 clothing. The machine broke innumerable haulage records and its availability was extremely high. Sadly, although its purpose had been served the locomotive was written-off after an accident during 1967. Here DP2 speeds through North Wembley with the 19.15 Euston to Perth in June 1962. *M. Pope*

Right: No D0260 *Lion*, forerunner of the Class 47s was built by a consortium of the Birmingham Railway Carriage & Wagon Company, Associated Electrical Industries Limited and Sulzer Bros (London) Limited. Introduced in 1962 the prototype is seen here ascending the Lickey Bank near Bromsgrove with a 16-coach, 495ton load. The white livery was striking to say the least. *IAL*

Below right: The superb 4,000hp Hawker Siddeley/Brush locomotive No HS4000 *Kestrel* was introduced in 1968. It is here seen at Wigan North Western working a Crewe to Carlisle test train on 8 May 1968. Sadly, this stylish machine was regauged and sold to Russia in 1971. *David Wharton*

D0280
0000

1T 60
WIGAN Nº

Class 15

Above: The British Thompson-Houston Type 1s, later known as Class 15, lasted from 1957 to 1971. As with many early diesel classes the amount of railway traffic suitable for 800hp locomotives dwindled considerably shortly after they were built. Here No D8206 runs along the North London line near West Hampstead with a train of vans and milk tanks for Kensington, in June 1969.
John Cooper-Smith

Class 17

Above: Over 100 of the twin-engined 900hp Class 17 'Claytons' were built from 1962 onwards. Most examples were to be found in the North of England and in Scotland. Except for the few examples sold to outside industry the class was extinct by 1972. On Maryport and Carlisle metals at Bullgill in Cumbria two examples are pulling hard at the head of a train from Workington. *P. W. Robinson*

Class 20

Top: A truly 'vintage' diesel scene at London's Euston station. Long before rebuilding and the appearance of overhead catenary a Class 20 in original green livery shunts parcels vans. The date is 21 October 1961 and the locomotive is No D8001 (now No 20.001). *M. Mensing*

Above: A typical North London scene from the early 1960s with Class 20 No D8015 (now 20.015) running past Brondesbury with a mixed freight. At this time a large number of these locomotives were allocated to Devons Road, Bow, and this accounted for their inter-regional travels around the Capital. *BR*

Above: The LMR allocation of Class 20s is now based at Toton depot in the East Midlands. They tend to work mainly on freights comprising older generation goods wagons. Nos 20.182 and 20.197 come off the Stoke on Trent line at North Staffordshire Junction with a Stoke to Toton freight on 5 August 1980. *A. O. Wynn*

Left: In recent years the Class 20s have usually worked in multiple to produce 2,000hp and to increase the brake force, thereby enhancing the 'stopping and starting business'. Two locomotives are not really required for this light load of coal seen with Nos 20.187 and 20.171 passing the Woodville Disposal Point sidings whilst working 'wrong line' to Overseal Sidings on 16 June 1980. *C. J. Tuffs*

Top right: At Blackwell Sidings, near the depot of Westhouses, Nos 20.071 and 20.142 await their path with a loaded train of 16ton wagons from one of the many East Midland pits. Even in this area of heavy freight traffic, sidings are seriously underused. *Colin Marsden*

Centre right: A popular location for enthusiasts is Blackwell Junction where trains from Westhouses join the Erewash Valley line. The 'board' is off for Nos 20.112 and 20.228 as they get to grips with a northbound coal train on 13 December 1979. *Colin Marsden*

Right: Nos 20.159 and 20.044 swing off the Leicester to Burton via Coalville line to visit Drakelow Power station via Drakelow East curve on 11 April 1980. The majority of coal trains serving power stations are now converted to the merry-go-round system but Drakelow can still accept these early 21ton coal hopper wagons. *Colin Marsden*

20 142

20112

Above: Nos 20.153 and 20.158 were photographed while doing business with the National Coal Board at New Hucknall Colliery, Huthwaite, Nottinghamshire, on 7 March 1980. The winding wheels above the mine shafts can be seen in the background. *Roger Kaye*

Left: One of the older Class 20s with route indicator discs, No 20.064, leads similarly fitted No 20.047, as they pass a clear signal at Glendon North Junction which indicates that the pair are destined for the slow road with their Toton to Wellingborough coal train. *F. R. Kerr*

Below left: Every summer Saturday scores of enthusiasts interested in haulage by freight locomotives converge on the Derby area to see if Class 20s have been diagrammed to work holiday extras. These enthusiasts have 'scored' with Nos 20.037 and 20.193 on the 13.02 Skegness-Derby, passing Beeston on 27 May 1978. *Norman E. Preedy*

Class 23

Above: The Class 23s, known as 'Baby Deltics', were employed on the Eastern Region, mainly on the GN suburban services. They were withdrawn during 1971 but one example, No D5901, survived for some time for experimental use by the Railway Technical Centre at Derby, bringing this type to the London Midland Region for the first time. Here No D5901 passes Coseley and Deepfields with a test train bound for Crewe on 19 February 1973. *Geoffrey Bannister*

Below: No D5901 ended its days at Derby, where it was photographed on 27 August 1975. It retained the original two-tone green livery with small yellow warning panels until the end. *John Vaughan*

Class 24

Left: In the days of green locomotives and maroon coaches one of the 'Type 2' Class 24s No D5147 (later 24.147) leaves Preston in Lancashire with a Saturdays-only train for the popular resort of Blackpool. Note the signalbox and semaphore signals which have now gone. *Norman E. Preedy*

Below: It is hard to imagine that this is now a place where Class 86/2s rush under overhead wires with Birmingham to Euston expresses. Long before such happenings, on 2 May 1963, No D5005 accelerates its five maroon compartment coaches out of Hampton-in-Arden with the 17.26 Birmingham New Street-Coventry local. *M. Mensing*

Right: Bescot in the Birmingham Division once had a sizeable allocation of Class 24s. However by 19 April 1977, when this photograph was taken, they were something of a rarity, with only about a dozen runners, and those mostly based at Crewe. A late survivor, No 24.063 rumbles through Bescot with a van train on its way to Walsall. *Geoff Dowling*

Below right: The section of the Much Wenlock branch, between Lightmoor Junction and Horsehay is retained to serve the Horsehay Ironworks which manufactures large items of steelwork. At Horsehay Goods Yard No D5137 is about to start out on the long journey to Motherwell in Scotland with an out of gauge load, a bridge girder, from the Horsehay Works, on 2 September 1971. *Geoffrey Bannister*

D 5137

9T11

Top left: Accelerating away from Madeley Junction with an Ironbridge CEGB Power Station to Ellesmere Port empty tanker train is No D5061 on 1 April 1970. Note the rarely used gangway connection in the centre of the cab. *Geoffrey Bannister*

Centre left: A pleasant photograph of an unusual train near Cosford between Wolverhampton and Shrewsbury. No D5078 (24.078) is hauling the massive Bescot breakdown crane back to base after re-railing a wagon at Lightmoor Junction on the branch to Ironbridge Power Station. *Geoffrey Bannister*

Left: Signs of heavy rains at Norton Colliery as water gently laps against the ballast supporting Class 24 No 5134 (No 24.134) and its coal train bound for Stoke-on-Trent on 8 December 1973. It is interesting to see that the pre-grouping practice of painting the owner's name on the wagons has been perpetuated by the Central Electricity Generating Board. *C. Plant*

Top: 'Double stamps' at Kidsgrove, where the Stoke to Manchester line leaves the Crewe lines, as two Sulzer 1,160hp engines are apparently required to move a long coal train from the Potteries area to Crewe on 17 April 1975. The locomotives are Nos 24.143 and 24.037. *Philip Hawkins*

Above: Along the Flintshire (now Clwyd) coastline near Bagillt runs No 5058 with an up freight on 21 March 1973. There were 151 Class 24s built, their life spanned 22 years and they made appearances on every region of BR. *A. W. Hobson*

Top: A great occasion when enthusiasts had their last opportunity to travel behind a Class 24 was 7 October 1978 when the RPPR 'Conway Consort' ran from Paddington to Blaenau Ffestiniog. No 24.082 headed the train and Class 40 No 40.113 assisted at the rear, banking the train to Blaenau where this photograph was taken. *John Vaughan*

Above: Another special to Blaenau, which featured No 24.082, occurred on 5 April 1978 when the locomotive was double headed by Class 25 No 25.043, nearest the camera. The train was a BR advertised excursion (Adex) from Brighton and is seen here at Llanrwst, one of the passing places on the long single line branch. *Bill Walker*

Above right: Cattle wagons such as those included in this mixed freight on the Caernarvon branch, have disappeared from the railway scene. When combined with a now extinct Class 24 on a branch line which has been closed and lifted the result is a nostalgic scene. No D5077 is the locomotive seen leaving Caernarvon on 30 March 1967. *A. W. Hobson*

Right: At Valley only a few miles from Holyhead No 24.035 regains the main line with a freight from Mold Junction on 20 January 1978. The 1,160hp Class 24s had a strong foothold in North Wales which continued almost until their extinction during 1980. *Larry Goddard*

Class 25

Left: Although the Cambrian lines are now under LMR control they are steeped in the traditions of the Great Western Railway. The signals here at Porthmadog goods yard are certainly of pure GWR ancestry. It is sad to reflect that all freight trains north of Tywyn have been withdrawn following the discovery of defects in Barmouth bridge and the few firms using rail freight services have now made other arrangements. The last regular freight traffic beyond Tywyn was gunpowder destined for Penrhyndeudraeth, and No 25.273 is seen with the unusual gunpowder vans, also of GWR origin, in June 1977. *John Vaughan*

Centre left: At Penrhyndeudraeth a short train of gunpowder vans is marshalled between barrier wagons in the attractive Cambrian Railways station. Note the wagon weighbridge on the left. On 10 May 1973 No D5142 leaves with 7J16, the 14.06 Portmadoc to Shrewsbury, Coton Hill Yard goods. *Geoffrey Bannister*

Below: The old Cambrian main line turns southwards from Dovey Junction to Aberystwyth. This view of Aberystwyth is unusual in that it shows the narrow gauge Vale of Rheidol line on the left of the picture. No 25.194 is leaving with the thrice weekly goods on 24 June 1980. *John Vaughan*

Right: Llanfairpwllgwyngyllgogerychwyrnd-robwllllantysiliogogogoch — need one say more? Class 25 No 25.209 is about to leave the Isle of Anglesey with an up freight on 31 May 1978. The passengers are likely to have quite a wait for their train while the goods leaves the long signalling section. *Brian Morrison*

Below right: London Euston sees daily Class 25 action with one of the Willesden-based locomotives shunting parcels vans. On a gloomy 19 April 1975 No 25.072 is attached to one of the delightful Western Region Siphon G vans whilst Class 86/2 No 86.254 lurks in the background. *Stanley Creer*

Left: Making a change from the usual West Coast main line electrics is No 25.174 running down the slow lines north of Watford with a string of 14 cement wagons. These locomotives are now becoming surplus and being withdrawn as a result of dwindling freight traffic caused by the general economic 'recession'. *Brian Morrison*

Below left: The Stewartby to Manchester and Liverpool 'Fletliner', heavily loaded with bricks necessitated double-heading by Class 25s on 8 July 1977. The 2,500hp was provided by Nos 25.258 and 25.145 here seen leaving Bedford. The lines on the right are the fast roads which by-pass Bedford station. On the slow line to the left is a rake of diesel-hydraulic dmus, soon to be displaced by electrification and this view is now partially obscured by overhead wires. *I. J. Hodson*

Above right: Class 25s are seen in nearly every corner of the London Midland Region. Locomotives of this class are sometimes employed on enthusiasts' specials such as the DAA/DEG 'North West Rambler' tour of 13 January 1979. The train is traversing the ex-LNWR Ocker Hill to Wednesbury branch in crisp wintry conditions. *Geoffrey Bannister*

Centre right: A diesel traction fan jots Nos 25.321/5 in his notebook as they roll through Long Eaton with the 12.58 Skegness-Derby on 4 August 1978. The Class 25s, like the Class 20s, tend to be used for passenger work most often on summer Saturday extras. *Norman E. Preedy*

Below: An unusual mixture pairing of Class 25 and 40 locomotives. An excursion on Bank Holiday Monday 1977 pauses at Manchester Victoria station to change crews before continuing in an easterly direction. Both classes are capable of working in multiple and have the common 'blue star' coupling code. *Frank Wilde*

Left: Climbing through the Pennines and about to enter Standedge Tunnel with the 09.00 Llandudno to York on 14 July 1979 is No 25.103 from Wigan Springs Branch. Even with a modest 6-coach load the run presents quite a challenge to the small diesel, especially when one considers that the maximum engine rating of 1,250hp is reduced to about 950hp at the rail. *David Flitcroft*

Below: A complex of lines at Wednesbury in the Black Country as seen on 19 July 1977. Behind No 25.292 the lines to the right go to Dudley and Stourbridge, to the left to Wednesbury Steel Terminal and straight on to Ocker Hill Power Station. *Geoff Dowling*

Right: Toton-based No 25.135 approaches the vast Toton yard with a down freight of 4-wheeled vans. The Sulzer 6LDA28B diesel engine provides ample power for this type of traffic in this area which, at least on the primary routes, is devoid of any long and severe gradients. *John Vaughan*

Below right: On 20 August 1980 No 25.139 takes the Derby line at Clay Cross Junction, just inside the London Midland Region boundary near Chesterfield, with a train formed mainly of coal empties. *John Vaughan*

25119

Left: The lines north of Liverpool are sadly underphotographed. Here, No 25.119, fitted with miniature snow ploughs, has just entered Southport goods yard and will shortly be indulging in some light shunting. *Gavin Morrison*

Below left: On 29 September 1969 an unidentified Class 25 ambles along the branch line from Stourport-on-Severn to Hartlebury with coal empties from Stourport Power Station. The branch passenger services were withdrawn from 5 January 1970. *John Vaughan*

Right: The Class 25s have regular turns on passenger services between Crewe and South Wales. No 25.073 accelerates the 12.25 from Crewe to Cardiff past Bayston Hill south of Shrewsbury on 12 September 1979. Although traffic on this line increases in the summer, the basic service is sparse, even with the Central Wales line trains which share the track north of Craven Arms, the 'border' between the Western and London Midland Regions. *Roger Kaye*

Below: There are considerable volumes of mineral traffic between Northwich in Cheshire and Chinley in Derbyshire, the large quarries of the Peak District serving the needs of industry, especially the ICI installations near Northwich. Standing at Northwich station with large empty air-braked hopper wagons is No 25.196. *Graham Scott-Lowe*

Left: At the other end of the run from the Northwich area is Chinley. From here freight only lines diverge to a number of limestone quarries in the Peak District east of Buxton. A string of empty hoppers rattle behind No 25.148 near Chinley on 21 September 1976. *Brian Morrison*

Below: Spectacular country surrounds Nos 25.113 and 25.157 as they thread the cutting near Frodsham with a Penyfford-Gumnie company train on 9 May 1979. The wagon covers not only stop dust flying and contents spilling but protect the load from the elements. *David N. Clough*

Right: The Potteries area around Stoke-on-Trent still enjoys plenty of freight activity, although in common with most areas the uneconomic wagon-load freights are giving way to block trains. There is not much bulk in these four empty coal wagons attached to No 25.032 at Cockshute Sidings, Stoke, photographed on 18 May 1979. *A. O. Wynn*

Below right: On North Staffordshire or 'Knotty' lines, not far from the late-lamented Leek & Manifold Railway, a smart brace of Class 25s Nos 25.194 and 25.195 are seen running down from Cauldron Low Quarry on 1 June 1979. The driver is about to relinquish the single-line token at Leek Brook Junction before continuing to Stoke-on-Trent. *Les Nixon*

25 194

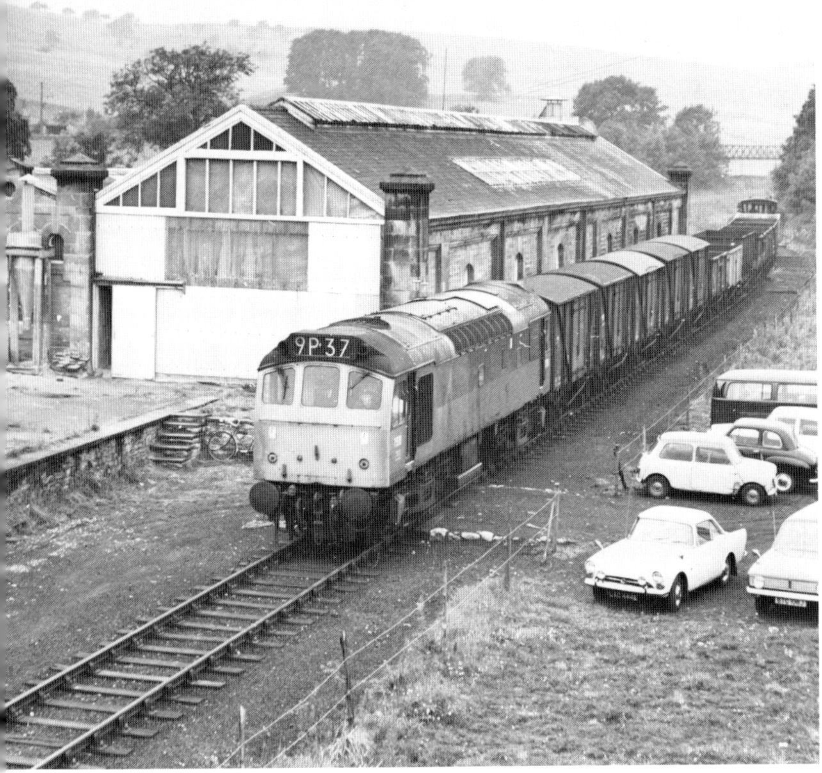

Left: The old station at Kirkby Stephen East has seen far better days than in this September 1971 photograph. No 7569 (now 25.219) in two tone green livery, works a Carlisle to Merrygill freight past this old outpost of the North Eastern Railway. *Stanley Creer*

Below: February on the Settle and Carlisle line is not for the faint-hearted. In cold clear weather No D7673 disturbs the peace of the hills near Horton-in-Ribblesdale with a down class 8 freight, on 14 February 1970. *Gavin Morrison*

Right: The vast LMR territory extends to the shores of Cumbria. No 25.292 was photographed at Beckermet iron ore mine on 10 September 1980 just before the line closed. The loaded wagons will be taken down to Workington Iron & Steel Works on the coast. *Dr J. McGregor*

Class 26

Above: Scottish Region allocated No 26.012 stands at Carlisle station during the evening of 6 June 1979, after making a rare trip across the border with a vans train from Glasgow. *Colin Marsden*

Class 28

Top: The unique Metro-Vick Co-Bos (6 wheels on one bogie and 4 on the other) were introduced in 1958 and only 20 were built. The class was soon banished to a quiet corner of Cumbria, working out of Barrow-in-Furness. Their short working life ended in 1968, having only just outlived the steam engine on BR. No D5708 heads a down block oil train through the Furness platforms at Carnforth on 26 August 1966. *A. W. Hobson*

Above: With at least four railwaymen in the driving cab No D5713 passes Chinley South Junction with a long train of empty ICI limestone hopper wagons. The 8-cylinder Crossley engine developed 1,200hp but like so many early classes they were not adopted as standard BR motive power. One reason could have been their massive weight, at 98tons, some 20 to 25tons heavier than a Class 25. *John Clarke*

Class 31

Top: One of Finsbury Park's Class 31s, with waistband stripe, has just crossed from the Eastern Region to the London Midland at Canonbury Junction to join the North London line. No 31.402 was photographed on 16 May 1979 with a very mixed load which included parcels vans and empty sleeping cars. *Les Bertram*

Above: These two Stratford-based Class 31s Nos 31.185 and 31.138 are using a stretch of London Midland track on the North London line near Hampstead Heath to cross from the Eastern Region to either the Southern or Western Regions with a heavy train of oil tankers, probably from Ripple Lane, on 16 April 1980. *Michael J. Collins*

Top: At precisely 11.14 on 19 June 1980 No 31.275 runs down the Erewash Valley line with a ballast train. Class 31s are not allocated to the LMR and thus they only appear on through inter-regional workings. Photographs of the class on the LMR are not rare but neither are they particularly common, except for locations in the East Midlands where they often work across the boundary. *John Vaughan*

Above: Two permanent way workers in high visibility jackets look on with interest as No 31.145 runs into the vast Toton marshalling yard with a wide variety of ballast hopper wagons in tow on 12 November 1979. *John Vaughan*

Top: Two Class 31s are able to produce a power output equivalent to a Type 4 locomotive. During 1976/77 the Western Region was often short of motive power and the 06.45 from Paddington to Birmingham New Street was then hauled by a pair of Class 31s. In 1976 Nos 31.257 and 31.230 emerge from the depths of the tunnel and enter New Street with such a working. *John Vaughan*

Above: A busy scene at Stenson Junction south of Derby. An Old Oak Common-based Class 31, No 31.117, with large numerals and no headcode panel, is far from home, and heading south with steel coil having come off the freight only line from the Nottingham area. On the right two Class 20s have just visited Willington Power Station. *John Vaughan*

Left: Another Class 31 with headcode discs rather than a panel is No 31.105, seen here passing Melton Mowbray with a steel train from Lackenby, Teesside to Corby on 27 June 1980. *Stanley Creer*

Below left: By far the most regular Class 31 workings on the LMR are on the Birmingham to Norwich through trains. The trains always comprise either 5 or 6 coaches and a MkI BG van requiring locomotives with a steam heating capability. No 31.229 arrives at Leicester on 16 August 1978 with the 13.17 from Norwich. *Norman E. Preedy*

Right: With its 12-cylinder, 1,470hp English Electric engine working hard No 31.236 nears Nuneaton on a sunny 19 May 1977 with the 07.54 Norwich-Birmingham New Street. *Kevin Lane*

Below: At Whitacre Junction near Water Orton No 31.173 rattles over the points with seven bogies forming the 16.38 Birmingham to Norwich on 27 May 1980. The lines to the right go to a nearby power station. This is a popular diversionary route when there is Sunday engineers' possession on the line between Birmingham and Rugby. *John Chalcraft*

No 31.164 gets a morning Norwich to Birmingham train under way at Water Orton on 18 February 1980. This route is one of the few remaining cross country classics and the 175$\frac{3}{4}$ mile journey takes almost four hours with semi-fast running. *Les Nixon*

Class 33

Top: Although the Southern Region Class 33s take over most inter-regional trains at Willesden for the journey round the West London Extension to the Clapham area they occasionally appear on miscellaneous workings through to the LMR. On such a journey No 33.053 powers a train of continental refrigerated vans through Kensington Olympia in June 1976. *John Vaughan*

Above: Under the catenary at Canley, on the outskirts of Coventry, with a Birmingham-bound cement train are Nos 33.037 and 33.034 on 30 June 1980. During 1980 this was a regular turn for the 'Comptons' whereas other workings into the area, for example on through passenger trains from Poole and Weymouth, were very irregular. *Geoff Dowling*

Left: Another view of the Handsworth (Birmingham) to Northfleet, Kent, cement train, this time hauled by a single locomotive, No 33.039, near Cropredy on 28 August 1980. *Roger Kaye*

Below: The 8-cylinder Sulzer-engined Class 33s sometimes work BR Adex specials to the Birmingham area and occasionally work throughout on inter-regional trains when Reading cannot find alternative motive power. However, workings through to Wolverhampton are most unusual. Here No 33.019 comes to a halt at Wolverhampton High Level with the 09.35 extra from Poole on 8 April 1980. *Norman E. Preedy*

Class 35

Top: The Class 35 Beyer-Peacock 'Hymeks' are now extinct on BR. These chunky 1,700hp diesel-hydraulics, based on the Western Region, were sometimes seen as far afield as Crewe but the only regular sorties were on the LM-controlled West London line. No D7028 runs past Earls Court Junction on a Western Region to Southern Region freight on 7 June 1969. *John Cooper-Smith*

Above: Another 'Hymek'-hauled inter-regional goods seen on the West London line but this time at Kensington Olympia. Note the strong Western Region influence with lower quadrant semaphore signals. The locomotive is No D7036 and the date 6 August 1969. *John Cooper-Smith*

Class 37

Left: As with the Class 31s, the London Midland Region does not have an allocation of Class 37s and most sightings on the LM are at the head of trains which have originated on another region. On full power for the climb to Camp Hill on the Birmingham New Street avoiding line is No 37.132 with a freight train of steel girders. *Geoff Dowling*

Below: One of the exceptions to the general rule takes place on the Lickey incline where a pair of Class 37s often perform banking duties. However, this may be splitting hairs because the Western/London Midland Region boundary is just before Blackwell summit. Just yards into the LM Region is this Thornaby-based Class 37 No 37.072 which had paused at the summit with a single brake van on 15 August 1978. *John Vaughan*

Above right: Piling on the amps, Canton-based No 37.230 speeds southwards with a block tank train near Wichnor Junction south of Burton-on-Trent, photographed in late evening sunshine on 19 June 1980. These fine machines have one of the highest availability records on British Rail. *John Vaughan*

Right: This Class 6 tanker train from Waterston in Dyfed (formerly Pembrokeshire) to Albion in the Birmingham area is a very long haul. Nos D6990 and D6997 (now 37.290/97) show they are pulling hard by covering Coseley station with exhaust on 17 February 1973. *Geoffrey Bannister*

Below right: With wagons to be seen in every direction No 37.086 negotiates Toton Yard in November 1979 with a down ballast working, whilst a pair of Class 20s bring in a long coal train from the East Midlands coalfields. In the right background a 'Peak' has just come off Toton shed. *John Vaughan*

37290

Way out
6M53

Above: BREL Doncaster Works overhauls most of the Class 37s but Crewe Works takes on a few of the class from time to time. No 37.112 ascends from Basford Hall (Middle) Sorting Sidings with a test train which it will haul to Church Stretton. This is its first run ex-works hence its splendid condition. *Barry J. Nicolle*

Left: Lovely Pennine scenery just east of Todmorden overlooks No 6735 (later 37.035) on 8E89 Rose Grove to Healey Mills coal empties on 2 June 1971. *John Cooper-Smith*

Below left: Except for seasonal passenger extras from Yorkshire to the Lancashire coast resorts (mainly Blackpool) the line over Copy Pit is freight-only. Creeping off the line at Hall Royd Junction on 2 August 1980 is No 37.209 on the 13.55 (SO) Blackpool to Sheffield. *Steve Turner*

Above: Eight large 100ton bogie tanks make up a respectable load for No 37.074 as it attacks the climb to Copy Pit. These trains are normally manned by Eastern Region crews who do an 'out and back' turn in a single shift. Photographed on 23 August 1978. *G. Roose*

Right: The sight of No 37.016 at Peak Forest on 24 June 1980 was most unusual. The train is the afternoon Hindlow to Glazebrook which is seen coming out of Ashwood Dale at Peak Forest Junction. The abandoned line to the left went to Bakewell and Derby; the passenger service being withdrawn from 6 March 1967. *Roger Kaye*

Class 40

Above left: A photograph from the interesting period between the end of steam and the beginning of electrification on the WCML. A green Class 40 on maroon stock gets to grips with Camden Bank on the 07.45 Euston to Manchester express on 31 August 1964. The locomotive, No D377, was one of the later batches of Class 40s built with centrally-placed headcode panel. *Brian Stephenson*

Left: A full 12-coach load for 2,000hp Class 40 No D380 on 22 July 1967 at Llandudno Junction. Such loadings were common on summer Saturdays in order to provide seating accommodation for the large numbers of holidaymakers. The train is the 11.40 Holyhead to Euston. *A. W. Hobson*

Top: Class 40s are still regular performers along the North Wales coast, and summer Saturdays still see a near invasion of the 23-year-old 'whistlers'. Saturday 12 July 1980 produced an added attraction in the shape of No 40.174 on a Willesden to Holyhead freightliner, photographed passing Sandycroft. *Geoff Dowling*

Above: The fine old station at Bangor is located in a picturesque setting between two tunnels. In the pre-holiday season BR often runs 'look and book' holiday preview specials to Bangor at very reasonable prices. On 19 April 1975 No 40.019 was employed on such a train and is seen here on the empty stock. *Stanley Creer*

Left: In the mid-1970s it was not unknown for up to three Class 40s to visit the Cambrian Coast on the same day but it is now rare to see even one. At Aberystwyth, still in green livery but with full yellow warning panel, is No 40.187 on a return excursion to Mexborough on 18 August 1974. *Norman E. Preedy*

Centre left: The seldom photographed junction at Helsby enjoys some activity on 4 November 1975. No 40.174 is coming off the Hooton line with 6F33, Stanlow to Cowley Hill (St Helens) tanks while a dmu for Rock Ferry pauses at the station. *David I. Rapson*

Below: A gem of a picture with a green Class 40 about to pass some long forgotten trackwork at Birkenhead Dock with a load from the past — the 18.30 Morpeth Dock to Crewe cattle train. Thirteen years have passed since this scene of bygone trains and structures was photographed on Sunday 20 August 1967. *Ian Krause*

Right: A rather bleak day to show off one of the more attractive parts of Lancashire, but No 40.087 at Moore, near Warrington with a freight from the Wirral in June 1975 makes a fine sight. The Class 40s are ideal locomotives on long loose-coupled freights like this due to their great weight and consequent braking ability. Sadly the gradual demise of this sort of train in favour of the block-load air-braked vehicles will see the ranks of Class 40s seriously eroded in the next few years. *Philip Hawkins*

Below: Lets all go to the races — and over the years the 'Grand National' at Aintree has become almost an institution. Specials descend upon the Liverpool area in their dozens, many of them hauled by Class 40s for part of the journey. In the Spring of 1971 No 319 (40.119) was diagrammed for the 1Z76 special from Bridgwater in Somerset, photographed leaving Edge Hill. *Norman E. Preedy*

Left: The famous station at Rainhill photographed some five years before the 'Rocket 150' celebrations focused attention on the site. On 27 April 1975 No 40.026 worked 1E06, the 08.50 Liverpool to Newcastle, which is seen heading eastwards on its way to Manchester. In the background is the well-known 'skew bridge'.
David I. Rapson

Below: One of the main centres for the class in the north-west is Springs Branch depot at Wigan. 'SP' has an allocation of over 30 Class 40s which handle much of the freight in the area. One of the few examples with split headcode boxes, No 40.136, reverses into the depot with a Class 25 in tow on 7 March 1979. *John Vaughan*

Right: Woodley station to the west of Stockport is an important junction where the Woodhead and Hope Valley trans-Pennine routes are linked and where a freight-only line from Merseyside by-passes the City of Manchester. On 14 May 1979 No 40.131 rumbles through on a southbound steel train. *Norman E. Preedy*

Centre right: The once grand station at Chinley on the edge of the Peak District still sees plenty of freight traffic but with a few exceptions most of the Hope Valley passenger trains are formed by dmus. Limestone and cement are the mainstay of freight traffic and in this view No 40.110 eases out of the down loop with a cement train from Earl's Works, on 8 September 1980. *John Chalcraft*

Below: Guide Bridge, in the West Manchester area, is an important region for freight. The line through the station sees not only diesel hauled traffic but for the moment the 1,500V dc overhead electrics which run over the Woodhead route. Although most Manchester based Class 40s are allocated to Longsight shed, at weekends when there is very little freight traffic about, there are lines of Class 40s stabled at Guide Bridge. No 40.082 trundles a handful of ballast wagons through 'GU' on 25 February 1979. *Gavin Morrison*

Left: About 11 miles north-west of Manchester is Bolton. The surrounding area has suffered badly from mill and factory closures in recent years and it is possible to see miles of disused sidings, or sites where sidings were once located. Nevertheless the four-wheeled loose-coupled goods has not entirely vanished as can be seen in this June 1978 photograph of No 40.128 heading a southbound coal train past Moses Gate. *David Flitcroft*

Right: A most unusual sight on the busy double-track section of the WCML on 4 June 1979, was No 40.128 climbing towards Shap summit with a train of steel bars. The reason for the working was the closure of the Settle and Carlisle route due to late running engineering works. *Colin Marsden*

Left: Farther north on the LMR at Settle Junction No 40.100 shows a trace of exhaust smoke as it gets a freight underway in preparation for the long slog over the Settle and Carlisle route on 15 August 1979. Although the railway photographer can now wait on this route, sometimes for a couple of hours, without seeing a freight train — when it does turn up the odds will be on a Class 40 heading the train. *Les Nixon*

Centre left: The 131ton bulk and 69ft 6in length of the Class 40 is apparent in this profile taken on the Settle & Carlisle. No 40.020 is on a northbound freight on 29 August 1979 and the locomotive is interesting for two reasons. Firstly, like 23 of its sister engines it was once named after a famous ocean liner, in this case *Franconia*, of the Cunard Line. With the passage of time all nameplates have been removed or stolen however, and secondly, the gap between the vast bogies means that the boiler water tanks have been removed, although the actual boiler remains in situ to add to the weight available for adhesion. This means that the locomotive is normally used for freight haulage only. *John E. Oxley*

Right: Making music in the hills with its 16-cylinder engine working hard is No D333 (now 40.133) hammering past Grayrigg in July 1965 with an up freight. *John Cooper-Smith*

Class 42

Above: In the early days of dieselisation many passenger workings followed the same pattern as the steam-hauled services established by the pre-Nationalisation railway companies and this resulted in many interesting inter-regional locomotive workings. On the old GW/LNWR Joint line through Wellington, Shropshire, now under LMR control, Class 42 'Warship' diesel-hydraulic No D817 *Foxhound* works through from the Western Region with the 14.10 Paddington-Birkenhead on 27 August 1962. *M. Mensing*

Left: Nearby is the 'North and West' route through Shrewsbury, where No D813 *Enterprise* is seen on 1V58, the 15.10 Liverpool to Cardiff through train, on 23 June 1962. The Class 42s had Maybach engines whereas the Class 43 'Warships' had North British/MAN power units; the transmissions were also of a different manufacture. *John S. Whiteley*

Class 43

Above: Temeraire is a name now perpetuated on a Class 50 locomotive but back in 1962 it was carried by Class 43 No D851. The locomotive was unusually photographed at the south end of Crewe station waiting to take over a train destined for the West Country. By 1972 all of the 'Warships' had been withdrawn. During her 10-year life span *Temeraire* completed just over 700,000 miles. *Brian Harcsnape*

Right: Crewe at night, with No D863 *Warrior* waiting for the road after coming off the 12.45 Penzance to Glasgow through train which conveyed some carriages working from Plymouth to Liverpool. D863 is seen in green livery on 6 March 1964. *John Clarke*

Class 44

Above left: A vintage photograph of one of the original 'Peaks', later known as Class 44s, with the express passenger headcode discs as used in steam days. No D4 *Great Gable* in green livery builds up speed through Luton in September 1960. The last of these 1959-built 2,300hp machines was withdrawn in 1980. *John C. Baker*

Left: Like Class 40s, the Class 44s lost their nameplates over the years and in this view of No 44.005 the bolts which retained the plate can be detected above and to the right of the number. The locomotive, formerly *Cross Fell*, is running light engine through Walsall station after working a Toton to Bescot freight on 19 July 1977. *Geoff Dowling*

Above: Corby sees a fraction of the freight traffic it once did now that the BSC steelworks has closed. Bearing in mind that the town was deprived of passenger services as long ago as April 1966 Corby has suffered considerably and inhabitants must now rely on bus connections to the nearest stations, such as Peterborough or Kettering.
No 44.004 passes the disused platforms with a northbound goods on 14 April 1980.
Jim Wade

Right: No 44.004 again, but this time approaching Radcliffe-on-Trent with a train of mixed wagons bound for Toton. The locomotive had received some superficial damage in a derailment at Walsall. The photograph was taken on 19 June 1980 and by this time workings were so rare that to take a Class 44 in action gave a sense of achievement. *John Vaughan*

Left: A striking photograph, taken on 17 July 1974, of No 44.010 *Tryfan* winding a long haul of coal out of Toton Yard for Wellingborough. In the background two Class 08s sort out the profusion of wagons in the East Yard. *Philip Hawkins*

Below: One of the regular workings for the class during their final years was on Toton to Tinsley freights, especially it seemed, in the evenings. After it had been spruced up for a depot open day No 44.008 *Penyghent* looked attractive as it rolled a coal train past Doe Hill north of Westhouses in July 1979. *Roger Kaye*

Class 45

Top: The magnificent 1868 trainshed at St Pancras, pride of the Midland Railway, and now happily a listed building. Two Class 45s fitted with electric train heating (eth), Nos 45.117 and 45.108, pose in front of the stock for the 13.08 departure to Nottingham. However, No 45.117 was only being temporarily berthed at the platform due to line occupation. Photographed on 10 March 1980. *Brian Morrison*

Above: A photograph taken just before the unsightly electrification poles were erected on the St Pancras to Bedford section of the Midland main line. Class 45 No 45.133 passes a surviving semaphore signal gantry at Cricklewood with an up express on a frosty 2 January 1980. *Colin Marsden*

Above: A named Class 45/1 No 45.135 *3rd Carabinier* foresakes air-conditioned coaches for more mundane duties and climbs the 1 in 400 away from Elstree past now demolished signals with 8M41 empties for Toton. *Peter Dobson*

Left: A splendid view of the old order at Bedford with the staple power for the line, a Class 45, No 45.121, on Mk 1 stock, surrounded by a multitude of metal and wooden post LMR semaphore signals. Although taken as recently as Easter Monday 1977 the photograph can never be repeated. The train is a Derby to St Pancras stopper. *Alan N. Pierce*

Above right: A glimpse of the new scene finds No 45.146 under the wires of the Bedford-St Pancras electrification. The train is the 14.30 St Pancras-Sheffield and the date is 2 September 1979. *Les Bertram*

Right: 'All clear' on the up fast road at Harpenden Junction for a 'Peak' on parcels in January 1979. The locomotive is one fitted with a split headcode panel. Most of these are being replaced with a metal plate containing spot marker lights as they pass through the workshops for overhaul. *John Vaughan*

Above left: This study of Class 45 No 45.141 on the 15.00 Sheffield to St Pancras passing Finedon Road Yard, Wellingborough hauling a smart rake of air conditioned stock is a photograph with some impact. The yard is still in business and justifies the full time presence of a Class 08 shunter.
Colin Marsden

Left: Twin telegraph poles and upper quadrant signals have always been synonymous with former Midland Railway lines. The line south of Kettering is no exception as seen in this study of No 45.140 heading a Derby to London stopping train towards Wellingborough. *John Vaughan*

Above: At Sharnbrook the fast and slow lines separate and for a few miles go their own way. Passing the last crossover for some distance is No 45.117 on 2 June 1979 making its way to the East Midlands with the 13.12 from St Pancras. *Geoff Dowling*

Right: Poor-light action photography of a light seven coach 'flyer' set between Kettering and Wellingborough making for the Capital. The concrete sleepered track with welded rails on the fast lines contrasts with the wooden sleepered, jointed track of the adjacent slow lines. *John Vaughan*

Left: 'Peaks' and yet more 'Peaks' at Wigston South Junction, Leicester. No 45.015 comes off the Nuneaton line to join the main line to London with a train of side-tipping ballast wagons while a sister locomotive stands by, on 8 September 1978. *Les Nixon*

Below left: A Derby station panorama with No 45.122 leaving the former MR headquarters for London on 25 May 1978. The line was very late to receive air-conditioned coaches and even these examples were 'cascaded' from other lines where High Speed Trains had been introduced. *Les Nixon*

Right: Birds-eye view from Alfreton Tunnel of a Class 45 at Alfreton and Mansfield Parkway. Between Trent and Clay Cross Junctions, trains from St Pancras to the north can travel via Derby or the Erewash Valley line before rejoining the same route northwards through Chesterfield. This unidentified down train is on the Erewash Valley line, on 16 August 1978. *Les Nixon*

Below: Clay Cross Junction with signs warning drivers of up trains that the restriction is 65mph for the Erewash Valley and Nottingham line and 75mph on the Derby route. Sweeping off the Derby line is No 45.032 on the 07.30 Birmingham to Newcastle on 20 August 1980.
John Vaughan

Left: A sheep is lucky to escape with its life as No 45.039 *The Manchester Regiment* blasts out of Blea Moor Tunnel with the 10.20 Nottingham to Carlisle on 28 April 1978. Most of the few passenger workings over the Settle and Carlisle are in the hands of Class 45s or 47s. *John E. Oxley*

Below: The hardest part of the work has been done by No 45.053 as it rouses Kirkby Stephen on 9 June 1979 whilst powering the 10.25 express from Nottingham to Glasgow. *Colin Marsden*

Right: No 45.053 again, but this time many miles from the Settle and Carlisle, and leaving Liverpool Lime Street with the 15.10 to Newcastle on 16 April 1976. This was the period when, after the discontinuance of train head codes, all blinds were turned to show '0000'. *Paul Gerald*

Below right: Although the 'Peaks' are associated primarily with the Midland main line they are almost as common on North East to South West inter-regional workings. Rejoicing in the grand name of *The Royal Warwickshire Fusilier* No 45.104 passes Kings Norton station during rebuilding, on 16 August 1978 with the 18.10 departure from New Street, alias the 13.23 Edinburgh to Bristol Temple Meads. *John Vaughan*

00
00

Left: Freight trains no longer traverse the North Warwickshire line since the route was truncated south of Stratford-upon-Avon. On 14 June 1976 No 45.132 passes Hall Green with a freight for Gloucester, one of the few non-passenger workings on the line at that time. *Geoff Dowling*

Below: Birmingham New Street 'line up' with No 47.079 *G. J. Churchward* on the 09.20 Reading to Manchester, No 46.013 light engine, and on the right No 45.130 with the 08.30 Manchester to Swansea working, on 22 March 1980. *Brian Morrison*

Class 46

Top: The Class 46s are all dual-braked locomotives with steam heating only. They differ from the Class 45s in a number of ways, the most major item being the use of Brush traction motors in the Class 46s in place of the Crompton Parkinson type used in the Class 45s. This example, No 46.035 is on an ex-works running-in trial working as pilot from Derby to Leicester where it will be removed from the train, powered by No 45.116. This is a December 1976 scene. *Geoff Dowling*

Above: No 46.001 comes to a halt at Gresty Lane near Crewe with 7M86, the 21.50 SX St Blazey to Carlisle freight. Not surprisingly the train includes a number of china clay wagons, giving a clue to its Cornish origin. *Barry J. Nicolle*

Left: The allocation of Class 46s was divided between Gateshead and Plymouth Laira depots, although with the ever reducing number of steam-heated passenger trains the class will doubtless be used in increasing numbers on freight trains or withdrawn from service. No 46.034 nears Kenyon Cutting at Newton-le-Willows with a mineral train on 1 June 1980. *Brian Morrison*

Centre left: After a derailment at the top of the Lickey Incline in August 1978 No 46.020 was called upon to attend with the engineers' train. The locomotive is facing 'wrong line' with its bright yellow CM&EE coaches. *John Vaughan*

Below: This photograph taken just within the LMR boundary shows the superb countryside around Marsh Brook on the Shrewsbury to Hereford line. Laira-based No 46.022 has worked this train, the 08.45 Newquay to Manchester Saturdays only holiday train, throughout, on 22 September 1979. *Les Nixon*

Class 47

Above: All members of the large Class 47 fleet are maintained at the BREL Crewe Works. The works has not only overhauled the class for some years but they have converted some of the earlier examples to Class 47/7 push-pull operation for the Scottish Region, and others from steam heating to electric train heating. This resplendent member of the Class is just about to emerge from the main diesel electric shop. *John Vaughan*

Top: On the left, beside the Test House in front of the Paint Shop is No 47.124 which is just ex-works whilst a Class 20 stands on the right and has yet to be repainted; a September 1979 view. *John Vaughan*

Above: Still the Great Western Railway in everything but name is the London to Birmingham route via Banbury, although most of it now falls within LMR territory. The southern part of the line was, strictly speaking, a Great Western/Great Central Joint line but there is no doubt about the lower quadrant look in this photograph of High Wycombe with a Class 47 on the only locomotive-hauled down passenger train of the day now using the line, the 17.42 Paddington to Birmingham. *John Vaughan*

Top: Princes Risborough is a really grand old station which has seen far better days. Running through the station on the up through road where once sparkling GWR 'Kings' stormed by on two-hour Birmingham expresses is Class 47 No 47.220 with a rugby football special from Hull to Wembley on 3 May 1980. The old footbridge is now disused and derelict. *John Vaughan*

Above: London Midland semaphores took over at Banbury but a decision was then made to scrap the lot and install colour lights. With only the goods line signals remaining No 47.066 makes a really fine sight as it brakes for the Banbury stop with a Liverpool-Poole train on 12 April 1980. *John Vaughan*

Top: While most of the population sleeps No 47.555 *The Commonwealth Spirit* quietly and efficiently rolls through Saltley Trading Estate with an abbreviated Royal Train early on Sunday 20 July 1978. Note the white wheel rims and yellow axle boxes.
Geoff Dowling

Above: Longbridge gained substantially in importance when the Birmingham suburban services were revised to provide through trains from Lichfield City in the north to Longbridge in the south from the May 1978 timetable. The new Longbridge station was built near Northfield Junction. On 11 May 1978, among the builders debris, two 6-car dmus wait at the up and down platforms while No 47.134 rushes past with the 09.40 Edinburgh to Plymouth.
Les Bertram

Top: A regular Class 47 duty is to haul dead electric locomotives and their trains over diversionary routes on Sundays when the normal electrified lines are closed for engineering work. At Abbey Junction, Nuneaton, No 47.196 drags Class 86 No 86.248 and the 12.40 Euston to Wolverhampton towards Water Orton, on 4 May 1980. *John Chalcraft*

Above: Crossing the River Weaver at Frodsham is No 47.456 with a freight for Manchester, on 17 August 1978. Although the Class 47s are not the most popular locomotives with enthusiasts they are capable machines, equally at home on long-haul freights or on express passenger trains. Their cabs are very comfortable for crews and have armchairs and electric heaters. *Les Nixon*

Above: Very few photographs seem to be taken between Chester and Northwich especially in the attractive Delamere Forest east of Mouldsworth. No 47.260 is seen in a sylvan setting near Delamere with coal empties returning from Birkenhead on 7 June 1976. *Peter H. Hanson*

Left: The container wagons of yesteryear seem now to be quite amusing when compared with today's large bogie wagons. Even more unlikely is the destination of this train — Broad Street in London. The locomotive is No D1944 (now 47.501), and it is seen passing Menai Bridge station with the train which originated at Holyhead, on 15 April 1967. *A. W. Hobson*

Above right: Back lighting adds to the effectiveness of this picture as the driver of No 47.027 opens the controller to accelerate a line of eastbound tankers through Chester on 30 March 1978. *A. W. Hobson*

Right: Signalmen must have a splendid view from the unusual and impressive Chester No 6 signalbox. The box controls far fewer points and signals than it used to, but at least it is still in operation. No 47.480 passes by with little fuss on a down summer Saturdays-only extra on 26 August 1978. *Les Nixon*

CHESTER Nº 6

Above left: Heading a merry-go-round train underneath the electrified West Coast main line at Warrington Arpley is No 47.188. This operation is one of the most successful rail freight systems with almost continuous movement between the collieries of the NCB and the power stations, maximising the use of resources in both men and machinery. *Graham Scott-Lowe*

Left: Brush Class 47 on the Fylde. No 47.449 slows down for the Poulton-le-Fylde stop with the 15.20 Blackpool (North) to London Euston on 26 August 1979. The line to the right goes to the ICI chemical plants at Thornton and a power station at Wyre Dock. *Noel A. Machell*

Above: In its original two-tone green livery with small yellow warning panel No 1623 threads the Lune Gorge at Dillicar, near Tebay with an up goods on 12 May 1966. The well-known water troughs can be seen between the rails but they have since been removed and electrification has come. *Norman E. Preedy*

Right: A bird's-eye view deep into the cutting at Kenyon, near Newton-le-Willows on 1 June 1980. An unidentified Class 47 heads what is thought to be an excursion for Blackpool North towards Parkside East Junction. *Brian Morrison*

5000

Above left: Carlisle has always been a massive centre for railway activity with lines radiating in every direction and much of the traffic centres on Kingmoor depot and yard. A railfreight load of modern air-braked vehicles enters Kingmoor on 8 June 1979 with No 47.485 braking for the stop.
Colin Marsden

Left: The single exhaust outlet of its 12-cylinder 12LDA28C 2,580hp engine throws smoke into the air as No 47.419 fights to move the 11.05 Liverpool-York out of Manchester Victoria on 1 March 1980. The Class 25 on pilot and banking duty is No 25.168. *John Vaughan*

Below left: A panoramic view of the City of Manchester as No 47.554 climbs Collyhurst Bank towards Miles Platting with a set of Mk 1 coaches forming the 10.10 Liverpool-Newcastle. The coaches behind the locomotives are above Red Bank carriage sidings. *Graham Williams*

Above: With a typical Stalybridge backdrop of mills and chimneys No 47.107 passes over the occupied arches of the viaduct with a Liverpool to Newcastle express. Most of these trains are hauled by Class 47s but occasionally a Class 40, 46 or even a 'Deltic' appears. *Les Nixon*

Right: An interesting daily cross-country train is the Manchester to Harwich, Parkeston Quay, service. Almost any class of locomotive can appear but by sheer weight of numbers Class 47s tend to dominate. Climbing towards Chinley on 1 March 1980 is No 47.011 with a vintage LMSR-type parcels brake van next to the locomotive.
John Chalcraft

Left: A failure at New Mills South Junction on 16 April 1980. Class 25 No 25.285 expired with Northwich to Tunstead ICI hoppers and after some delay No 47.306 arrived to give assistance. The Class 25 is obviously not doing any work as the ensemble gets under way. *Noel Johnston*

Below: The LMR end of the Manchester-Sheffield via Woodhead route was being used for diversions on 30 December 1979. Passing Torside signalbox over snow covered sleepers is No 47.501 on the Sundays-only St Pancras to Manchester train. The future of the line is the subject of much speculation, and mid-1981 could see closure.
Steve Turner

Right: Another train diverted due to Sunday engineering works, this time on 6 April 1980. Routed over the Pennines via Todmorden, the 07.50 Newcastle-Liverpool with No 47.465 up front, will shortly pass from Yorkshire into Lancashire on what was once part of the Lancashire & Yorkshire Railway.
John Chalcraft

Below right: The third in a trio of diversions, this strikingly photographed Class 47 is crossing Dent Head viaduct on the Settle and Carlisle line with a Sunday Carlisle to Euston train, on 2 May 1976. The Class 47 will be kept hard at work with the 12-bogie load.
John Cooper-Smith

Above: With not a motor car or human being in sight a Class 47 has only sheep for company as it rides high on Arten Gill viaduct with a massive coal train for Carlisle in June 1975. *John Cooper-Smith*

Class 50

Above: No D432 in original condition with 1A58 Carlisle to Euston getting away from Lancaster in September 1969. The entire Class of 50 Class 50s were built at Newton-le-Willows during 1967 and 1968 in the Vulcan Foundry. The locomotives performed well and although availability left something to be desired they outpaced the Class 40s and 47s on the Anglo-Scottish expresses. *Stanley Creer*

Right: The Oxenholme of yesteryear with sidings, overall roof for the Windermere branch train, signalbox, semaphore signals and a diesel-hauled train. Most of these things have now gone with the march of progress. No D447 (now 50.047 *Swiftsure*) departs from the station with the 08.30 Carlisle to Euston semi-fast on 27 August 1969, in the period before these locomotives were fitted with jumper cables for mu operation. *A. W. Hobson*

1S75

Above left: No 423 (to become 50.023 *Howe*) heads a down express on Grayrigg bank north of Oxenholme on 8 September 1969. The following year was to see the introduction of double-heading with Class 50s on this line. The extra power certainly smoothed performance on the gradients over the fells between Carnforth and Carstairs. *Stanley Creer*

Left: Cynics would say that with 5,400hp available double-headed Class 50s should have been fast enough to raise a few eyebrows on the LMR. This is exactly what they did do, with 100mph-plus speeds and phenomenal hill climbing ability. Even with the 12 bogies seen here, Nos 426 and 446 make Shap look like a mole hill with the 14.00 Euston to Glasgow on 19 May 1977. Note the scar of the M6 Motorway under construction on the hillside beyond. *John Cooper-Smith*

Below left: A spectacle to behold on the Settle and Carlisle line was the sight of double 'Hoovers' on the diverted 11.55 Glasgow to Euston express descending to Blea Moor over Arten Gill viaduct in October 1971. *Stanley Creer*

Above: An exceptionally rare photograph of a Class 50 at Macclesfield. The overhead power had been switched off for engineering works on a Sunday in 1973 and No 440 was rostered to work 1H30 the 11.30 Euston to Manchester. *Martin Welch*

Right: Whilst allocated to the London Midland Region Class 50s occasionally strayed from the Euston-Glasgow workings. With Blackpool Tower behind, No 50.027 found itself at the seaside working a train to Birmingham on 14 September 1974. Such workings were not unknown but they were still unusual enough to make such a photograph a real 'scoop'. *F. R. Kerr*

Above: Having travelled via the Settle and Carlisle line and Clitheroe the diverted 09.00 Glasgow to Euston passes Hoghton, near Preston, in order to regain the WCML. No 50.017 was in charge when photographed on 9 March 1975. By this time some of the Class 50s were being transferred to the Western Region following electrification of the Euston to Glasgow route throughout. *David Flitcroft*

Left: One of the last duties of the Class while allocated to the LMR was on mgr workings between Ironbridge CEGB Power Station and Silverdale in the North Staffordshire coalfield. At Cannock Road Junction No 50.022 (later *Anson*) reverses on to the Bushbury spur before continuing towards Stoke-on-Trent, 8 April 1975. *Geoffrey Bannister*

Above right: After transfer to the Western Region Class 50s were only to be seen on the LMR on inter-regional trains, rarely proceeding beyond Birmingham New Street. During 1978 the class were all named after famous Warships. Penetrating the snow covered tracks at Leamington Spa with the 13.25 Birmingham-Paddington is No 50.016 *Barham* on 27 January 1979. *G. O. Swain*

Right: There is much to absorb in this photograph. No 50.038 *Formidable* is starting out with 13.25 Birmingham-Paddington, with an army of 'Hoover bashers' in the leading coaches. Note the Class 47 on the mgr empties from Didcot, a Moor Street to Stratford dmu approaching, a light Class 47 on the freight-only Camp Hill line, and finally the modern City of Birmingham skyline. The date is Good Friday 1980. *John Whitehouse*

Above: Waiting to take the 12.20 to Plymouth out of the murky depths of Birmingham New Street is No 50.007 *Hercules*. London Midland Region drivers at Saltley are now passed to drive the Class 50s and the locomotives therefore tend to spend more time in Britain's second city than in previous years. *John Vaughan*

Left: It has been the practice recently that Class 50s being returned to the Western Region after overhaul at Doncaster Works are diagrammed to work 1V93, the 09.50 Edinburgh to Plymouth from York. On 27 May 1980 one of the refurbished Class 50s No 50.047 *Swiftsure* with headlight and numerous other mechanical and electrical modifications arrives at Derby. *Norman E. Preedy*

Below left: The striking new BR livery applied experimentally to a Class 56 was first applied to a member of the Class 50 fleet when No 50.023 was outshopped in August 1980. No 50.003 *Temeraire* was the second locomotive so treated and it was photographed on its maiden run in revenue earning service at Derby on 26 September 1980, also on the 09.50 from Edinburgh. *Barry J. Nicolle*

Class 52

Above: The exciting days of early dieselisation are exemplified in this view of High Wycombe with a maroon 'Western' No D1001 *Western Pathfinder* finding a path through the trackwork with the 07.10 Shrewsbury to Paddington on 29 September 1962. In the siding is a 4-car Derby-built dmu. A total of 74 'Westerns', later designated Class 52, were built from 1961 but by February 1977 all had been withdrawn. *H. K. Harman*

Right: The sun didn't shine on the 'Westerns' for very long after this photograph was taken of No D1022 *Western Sentinel* speeding towards the Midlands at Solihull whilst heading the 16.05 Paddington to Birmingham New Street in May 1975. These fine 2,750hp diesel-hydraulics were treated by the LMR as the Class 50s are today — if they do turn up, send them back to the Western Region, quickly! *Geoff Dowling*

Left: Another early view taken at a time when the twin-engined diesel-hydraulic Class 52s visited Shrewsbury regularly. No D1033 *Western Trooper* backs on to the 08.55 Birkenhead-Paddington on 28 October 1963 after a steam locomotive had brought the train into Shrewsbury. In the background 'Hall' class 4-6-0 No 6995 *Benthall Hall* performs pilot duties. *R. Stephen*

Centre left: One of the last ever visits to the LMR of a Class 52, and certainly the last to Chester and Crewe, was on 29 January 1977 when RPPR ran the 'Western Memorial' Railtour from Paddington. No D1023 *Western Fusilier*, happily preserved by the National Railway Museum, was the motive power and it ran without missing a beat. Still adorned with a magnificent headboard, now in the author's collection, D1023 runs past Crewe station light engine towards the depot for refuelling. *John Vaughan*

Below: A rare photograph of a Class 52 on the Westbury, Wiltshire, to Leagrave stone train on its return journey along the Midland main line at Harpenden. No D1022 *Western Sentinel* had shunted at Luton and was on its way up on the slow lines. The train ran only twice per week but it was finally caught on film on 21 September 1976. *John Vaughan*

Class 55

Above: An additional view of the 'Deltic' prototype is included here for the sake of comparison. Passing the fascinating old transporter bridge at Runcorn on the Liverpool to London line in November 1958 is the original 1955 3,300hp *Deltic*. The locomotive is now preserved in the Science Museum in London. *IAL*

Right: A Finsbury Park Class 55 No 55.018 *Ballymoss* worked into Liverpool Lime Street with a train from York on 8 September 1979 much to the delight of railway enthusiasts who witnessed the sight. The working of a 'Deltic' was not unique but the 'FP' locomotive with white window surrounds made all the difference. It was photographed at Lime Street prior to returning with an afternoon train. *Gavin Morrison*

Above: Full marks to the photographer, firstly for being on Stockport station at 00.51 in the rain, and secondly, for taking such a fine picture of No 55.010 *The King's Own Scottish Borderer* on the 22.50 Shrewsbury to York overnight train, on 29 December 1978. *B. Watkins*

Below: This Class 55 was specially requested by BR Sheffield in conjunction with an Adex trip for railway enthusiasts from Chesterfield to Carlisle and Carnforth on 10 July 1977. No 55.007 *Pinza* arrives at Carnforth with more heads out of the window than seen on the majority of steam-hauled specials. *F. Wilde*

Class 56

Above: It is unusual to capture photographs of Class 56s other than on mgr or fly-ash trains. One exception is the Fordors-Cricklewood 'Easidispose' rubbish containers which were Class 56-hauled on 6 August 1979 when pictured coming through Luton. *Geoffrey D. Griffiths*

Right: Merry-go-round trains from the Coalville area mostly serve Didcot and Rugeley power stations. After arrival at Rugeley main line station No 56.060 runs round its train and crosses the viaduct at the east end of the station on 19 June 1980. It will have to reverse again before entering the power station. *John Vaughan*

Above: Swinging off the freight only line from Wichnor Junction and about to join the WCML is No 56.039 with a Coalville to Rugeley Power Station mgr train. The train is passing the old wooden crossing gates at Lichfield Trent Valley Junction Crossing on 30 August 1978. *Geoff Dowling*

Left: Nearly two years after the previous photograph was taken No 56.039 was still running between Coalville and Rugeley. Pity anybody beside the track on this blustery day as clouds of coal dust from the fully-loaded mgr hoppers blow across the countryside at Walton-upon-Trent on 19 June 1980. *John Vaughan*

Below: The Ruston Paxman engine in the Class 56 is rated at 3,250hp. The large 16-cylinder diesel engine is capable of producing more power but in the interests of long term reliability BR run the fleet in slightly 'derated' form. No 56.033 passes Branston, near Burton-on-Trent, with mgr empties from Rugeley to Mantle Lane on 15 September 1978. *A. Wynn*

Above: Returning from Radcliffe Power Station and entering Toton yard in April 1980 is a rather grimy No 56.027. The Class is employed almost exclusively on freight duties and they therefore do not take passenger rolling stock through the carriage washers. Consequently, unless a locomotive has recently been through works, or depot time is spent on cleaning they tend to run in poor external condition. *John Vaughan*

Right: A profile of No 56.059 at Mantle Lane, Coalville, showing one of the substantial six-wheel bogies and the original BR livery. The first 30 locomotives were built in Romania but a number of modifications to the batch have since been carried out by BREL.
John Vaughan

56036
44 007

56059

Left: A Doncaster-built locomotive, No 56.036, was the first BR locomotive to be painted in an experimental colour scheme which was later to be adopted as standard for other classes. No 56.036 stands beside one of the now extinct Class 44s, No 44.007, at Toton Diesel Depot on 23 February 1980. *Peter Gater*

Below left: This next sequence of three photographs shows No 56.059 on a run from Coalville to Bagworth on the freight only Knighton South Junction, Leicester, to Burton-on-Trent line to load its rake of 34 mgr wagons. The signal is off at Bardon Hill as the train rumbles towards Leicester. *John Vaughan*

Right: Having run round its train at Bagworth No 56.059 eases forward at about 2mph, using its special slow speed control, while it is loaded with coal which has been conveyed a considerable distance underground from the coal face. This is a distant view across nearby fields. *John Vaughan*

Below: After loading, the train pulls out of the sidings to join the main line at Bagworth. Note on the left of the photograph that severe mining subsidence has affected the track, especially the 'dip' behind the hedgerow. No 56.059 will return to Coalville and then make for either Didcot or Rugeley. All photos taken on 11 April 1980. *John Vaughan*

Class 73

Class 74

Top: It was rare for any of the Southern Region's electro-diesels to work on to the LMR except on the West London line. Here one of the small Class 73s, No E6039 (now 73.132), passes West Brompton on 14 August 1973 with the 13.27 Acton to Plumstead freight. The locomotive has a maximum power output of 1,600hp on electrified lines and 600hp from its auxiliary diesel engine alone. *John Scrace*

Above: The more powerful Class 74 electro-diesels of the SR are now extinct. No 74.008 runs past Kensington Olympia with seven six-wheeled milk vans for Acton Yard. These locomotives were rated at 2,552hp on electric traction but on these lines its Paxman diesel engine would be producing its maximum output of 650hp. *John Vaughan*

Multiple Units and other Diesel Classes

Top: The Metro-Cammell 1959-built 'Midland Pullman' diesel sets were very advanced for the period and although similarity to the IC125 High Speed Trains is mainly cosmetic the mode of operation was similar. Each power car employed a 1,000hp North British/MAN 12-cylinder pressure-charged diesel engine. They were introduced on the St Pancras to Manchester Central route at a time when the route was far quicker than the Euston to Piccadilly service, due partly to electrification work on the latter, and continued on the LMR until 1965/66 when displaced by electrified services. Note the Pullman Car Company crest on the blue and white livery. *British Rail*

Above: The prototype IC125 Class 252 power cars are now in use on the LMR working out of the Derby Technical Centre on a variety of test runs, mostly with HST and APT vehicles. No 252.001 is seen here in the Derby Locomotive Works of BREL where it was receiving attention on 6 September 1980. *Graham Scott-Lowe*

Top: At the time of preparation of this volume the IC125 trains ordered for the inter-regional north-east to south-west service had not been built and therefore High Speed Train appearances on the LMR were not common, being confined to post-works test runs. However, during the repair work after the Penmanshiel Tunnel collapse of 1979 ECML trains were diverted via the LMR to Carlisle. Here No 254.031 passes Blackrigg with a down express on 8 June 1979.
Colin Marsden

Above: No 254.023 keeps unusual company with No 87.019 *Sir Winston Churchill* at Carlisle on 17 May 1980 after being diverted via the LMR with a Kings Cross to Edinburgh train. The Guard can be seen strolling across the platform to relieve his colleague and he will probably continue to Carstairs.
Les Nixon

Left: A diesel 'oldie' at Shrewsbury when the station still boasted its train-shed roof. Ex-GWR diesel railcar No W32W producing 210bhp and built in 1940 leaves the station with the 16.20 to Bridgnorth on 1 September 1962. These vehicles were already living on borrowed time and were soon replaced by later generation dmus although the Severn Valley line through Bridgnorth closed in 1963 without seeing many of the newer units.
I. Bentley

Right: A line almost devoid of through locomotive-hauled trains is that from Bletchley to Bedford, and although freight including bricks and 'Easidispose' rubbish containers appears on both ends of the line very few freight trains run from one town to the other. The line is punctuated with brickworks such as this example at Lidlington with a Cravens two-car unit passing on the 13.10 Bletchley to Bedford St John's on 22 March 1980. *Les Bertram*

Below: The Cambrian Coast at its best as a 9-car Sunday Adex special leaves Barmouth as ecs for Machynlleth where the stock will be cleaned and watered, in June 1980. The train was to have been locomotive-hauled but weight restrictions on the wooden Barmouth Bridge caused the dmu to be substituted. The sun was shining on this day in a summer which was poor for UK holidaymaking. *John Vaughan*

ROCKFERRY
B

ROWE BROS
SHOW ROOMS
0000
BOLTON

Left: A service which ceased from 4 May 1975 was that from Runcorn to Helsby. This ageing Park Royal dmu was photographed near Frodsham on 24 April 1975 with the 18.13 from Runcorn, which worked through to Rockferry on the Wirral peninsula. *David I. Rapson*

Below left: Leaving the old Liverpool Exchange station, once the pride of the Lancashire and Yorkshire Railway, is the 12.57 to Bolton on 23 September 1976. Derby-built car No M52052 is leading as the train smokes its way out of the now closed station. *Brian Morrison*

Right: The sun penetrates the cutting deep in the City of Leicester to the south of the Midland Railway London Road station as a Swindon cross-country 3-car dmu leaves for Birmingham New Street on 8 September 1978. *Les Nixon*

Below: The Blackburn area is sorely underphotographed by enthusiasts, which is surprising when a fine all over roof like this survives. Passengers should have little trouble telling the time! A 2-car dmu is about to leave for Manchester Victoria on 12 March 1979. *Les Nixon*

Top: A cold and bleak prospect at Rochdale on 26 February 1977. Not only is there snow on the hills but the jointed track has seen better days, and although the old upper quadrant semaphores still do their job, the letters are gradually dropping off the Rochdale East Junction signalbox sign. A Rochdale-Oldham-Manchester dmu scuttles by. *Les Nixon*

Above: The latest in passenger and freight motive power on the LMR. Class 56 No 56.059 on 'Railfreight' hopper wagons passes APT set No 370.002 (being hauled by No 252.001) at Toton on 23 October 1980. Whilst the APT is powered by electricity there will always be a good variety of 'Diesels on the London Midland Region'. *C. Burnham*